JAZZIN' About
fun pieces for
ALTO SAXOPHONE

CONTENTS

PAM WEDGWOOD

FABER *ff* MUSIC

TO THE TEACHER

Jazzin' About is an original collection of material written in popular styles ranging from Rock to Ragtime.

The pieces are arranged in order of increasing difficulty and I hope that teachers will find this collection a useful addition to any teaching programme, providing a firm foundation for more advanced studies in this style of playing. Stimulating accompaniments for piano (or electric/electronic keyboard) will help the student to achieve scrupulous articulation of rhythmic patterns and familiarity with the feeling and characteristics of the music.

One of the most important aspects of teaching a musical instrument is to ensure that the student enjoys what he or she plays. The study of varied idioms will encourage the pupil to progress faster both technically and musically.

TO THE STUDENT

My primary reason for writing **Jazzin' About** is to give you an opportunity to play in popular styles while you are in the earlier stages of your musical development. Jazz, Rock, Blues and Ragtime are all part of our musical heritage and should be experienced along with more 'classically' orientated works. However, learning to master popular rhythms can be hard work as well as fun! Once you have learnt each phrase, try to put a little of your own expression and style into it. Persuade your friends to join in!

I hope that **Jazzin' About** will give you new satisfaction and enthusiasm for your instrument.

Happy Blowing!

Pamela Wedgwood.

© 1989 by Faber Music Ltd
First published in 1989 by Faber Music Ltd
Bloomsbury House 74–77 Great Russell Street London WC1B 3DA
Cover by Velladesign
Music engraved by Sambo Music Engraving Co
Printed in England by Caligraving Ltd
All rights reserved

ISBN10: 0-571-51054-X
EAN13: 978-0-571-51054-2

To buy Faber Music publications or to find out about the full range of titles available please contact your local retailer or Faber Music sales enquiries:

Faber Music Limited, Burnt Mill, Elizabeth Way, Harlow, CM20 2HX England
Tel: +44 (0) 1279 82 89 82   Fax: +44 (0) 1279 82 89 83
sales@fabermusic.com   fabermusic.com

1. Walk Tall

PAMELA WEDGWOOD

2

CODA

4

2. Moonglow

6

3.   Hot on the Line

* ossia (trombone)

4. Going Home

JAZZIN' ABOUT

ALTO SAX

1. Walk Tall

PAMELA WEDGWOOD

2. Moonglow

Quite slow, with feeling (♩ = 72)

3. Hot on the Line

Moderate blues tempo (♩ = 80)

4

4. Going Home

5. Are You Ready!

6. Tequila Sunrise

7.   Sometime Maybe

8. Ragamuffin

5.   Are You Ready!

6.   Tequila Sunrise

16

7. Sometime Maybe

8.   Ragamuffin

22